CONTROL YOUR HABITS, OWN YOUR LIFE.

Harry Benjamin

Table of contents

Prologue

Final Thoughts

PROLOGUE

This book starts where everything ended. You died. (A morbid start, I know.) You look at your grave and your weeping family. Your tombstone says, "Here lies (your name), who lived 100 years." Rain starts to pour, and your friends and family slowly go home.

You have nothing else to do but contemplate your life. You can do it honestly now. You've passed the point of no return. It's game over. Nothing bad can happen if you admit what you should or shouldn't have done in your years on Earth.

Ask yourself: Was I truly happy? Did I miss out on something? What did I want to do and didn't go for? What are my regrets about my life? Would I say yes to any opportunities I missed? Or no to some I accepted?

If you feel you have no regrets, you did everything you wanted, and there's nothing you'd do differently, try again. And be honest now. I'm fairly sure you would have some what-ifs hanging around. Otherwise you wouldn't be reading a self-help book. You're still hungry for something, you want to accomplish something, gather the courage to step up your game, to raise your standards. You name it.

There's nothing wrong about feeling this way. It would be worse if you thought, "Meh, there's nothing left on this planet that entices me." It can be hard to pinpoint what exactly we missed, and what exactly we'd like to go for without a wider perspective on who we are and who we want to be as people.

A good practice to identify this is something Stephen R. Covey mentions in his book The 7 Habits of Highly Effective People. Namely, write your eulogy. In the previous exercise we approached your life from a scarcity mindset – what you missed out on and could have done differently. Now let's turn the tables. Imagine that you lived your best life, true to your personal values. What did you accomplish? What were your greatest victories? What legacy did you leave behind? What will you be remembered for? What did your children think and say about you? And your friends? What were your life-guiding principles? Take a moment to think about these questions. It's better if you write them down and answer them in writing.

Have a clear picture on what matters to you before you start ruminating on missed chances. I missed out on something that might have been a great career opportunity. The biggest modeling agency contacted me in Hungary at the age of sixteen and offered me a job in the fashion industry. It may or may not have turned out to be a real lifelong chance, but I said no. I was not interested at all. Modeling, while it is glamorous and I have nothing against those beautiful people who do it, is something that is not in alignment with my values. It doesn't interest me. Will I toss and turn in my grave for this missed opportunity? Nope.

But there are other opportunities that I missed and now regret. I know this because I know my values. Before addressing your regrets, it is good to get in alignment with your core values so that you can objectively assess what was a real loss and what was a smart decision.

Before we move on, think about this: what are my core values? I don't want to put words in your mouth; figure your answer out for yourself. Here are my main values as an example. To me, belonging to someone (not somewhere) is extremely important. I highly value being safely attached to someone; an emphasis being on "safely." I hate drama, games, and tension. I also value challenges – I love being challenged and growing as a person as a result. At the same time, I love being able to challenge someone and help him or her grow. I value kindness doing good for goodness' sake. I could go on but let's stick to these three.

Knowing your core values is key to living a meaningful life. Otherwise, how do you know what to do? What habits to develop? What to fight and strive for? People who live their lives out of sync with their values can often get tired, demotivated, and even depressed. What's the point? This is a legitimate question they should answer as soon as possible. This proverbial point is the point. What's your "point?" Think about it.

Did I just hit you with my words? Ouch, Zoe, I am demotivated! And you just threw it bluntly into my face! Well, good. I'm happy I did it. What do you think now? Was it useful information? Do you know what to do now as a first step? Let me repeat it: find your core values.

What motivates you? What makes you excited for no reason? Or on the contrary, what gives you a great sense of fulfillment and peace? Find these answers and go for opportunities that serve them.

People don't realize they've missed key opportunities until they find their values. When you know who you are and what you want, take action. Go for the "point."

"I'd rather apologize than ask permission."

"It's better to regret what you have done than what you haven't." – Paul Arden

Keep these sayings in mind.

If you have a clear set of values, a vision of life (the eulogy), a priority list of well-defined goals, and a reasonable, healthy daily schedule for them, you can find the time, energy, even the money to say yes more and enjoy your life to the fullest!

Here is some good news. You're not dead. Not at all. You are very much alive, here in this moment, and you have many more decades until you contemplate your life from the grave. Just don't forget that day will come and every day it comes closer. This is the beauty of life – it's finite. You can never know when your last day will be. You'll never be younger or more beautiful than you are right now. You'll never have this moment again. You have time, but none to be wasted. Don't waste it with regrets and complaints arising from a lack of clarity.

How can you make your future better? By changing the things that led you to a dissatisfied present.

Life isn't very complicated, as far as the big picture goes. Our days are mostly repetitive – composed of routines. What we see on social media – the special moments, the highs, the giant Nutella pancakes and holidays at Bali – are just blinks of an eye, heightened moments of an otherwise normal life. Everybody's life is composed of routines most of the time. This is why it is so important to have good routines that serve your core values. Good routines help you get to those occasional highs that make life special. Also, good routines are the ones that keep regrets at a minimum in your life.

All the distractions and barriers that stand between you and your ability to build healthy routines should be removed.

One of the biggest roadblock usually is procrastination. The "I will do it tomorrow" mentality seems harmless, but in fact, it can do a lot of damage if you don't focus on overcoming it. The first part of the book will talk about procrastination – its causes, its types – and provide a detailed action plan for how to overcome it.

The second part of the book will give you a broad perspective on how to organize your day to be more productive. It will also cover how you can keep up your productivity, best practices to bring out the most in each day, and advice from the world's top entrepreneurs.

The third part of the book will discuss daily philosophies you can wrap your mindset around. Having a coherent philosophy for life can make you more accepting of death, among other things. Acknowledging the inevitability of death will also highlight what in life is worth fighting for. Those who live without the core values of life will desperately try to delay their deaths, because their improvised or "trend-oriented" values convinced them they were on the right track and that they had time. People who think they will live forever are more likely to waste their lives than those who understand that human life is perishable and our days are numbered.

1. PROCRASTINATION

Procrastination... This seemingly harmless habit can pretty much leave you on your deathbed with a life full of regrets.

Procrastination, if not done in excess, is a natural state of mind. There's nothing wrong with you; everybody does it. If somebody tells you that he or she doesn't procrastinate, it's a lie. In small doses, it can even be helpful. If you don't take a pause from time to time, you can burn out very quickly. But there's a level above which procrastination prevents you from taking action, moving forward, and living a quality life. You know, the more you do, the better you feel. In the following pages, I present the dark side of procrastination. If you can relate to any or many of the descriptions, think about how much your life would improve if you changed it.

Procrastination slows development, derails your progress toward your goals, and replaces action with stagnation. It is the gravedigger of success. The difference between success and failure is action. Procrastination is a highly motivated state. We are motivated to do nothing, to avoid difficulties, obstacles, and emotionally intolerable situations. Procrastination arises when we put our present self ahead of our future self, prioritizing immediate pleasure over long-term gratification.

"Motivation is what gets you started. Habit is what keeps you going." – Jim Rohn

Rachel knew she had to finish her assignment at the end of the month, but it was only the seventh. She knew she had a lot of time left. She was confident in her abilities and knew that she'd be able to finish the work in one week – worst case. So she didn't do anything for two weeks. As each day passed, she convinced herself more and more that she had time. Each day, she had to come up with better explanations and justifications.

When there was only a week left until the deadline, she rationalized that six days should also be enough for her to finish if she worked an extra hour each day. When only six days were left, something unexpected happened, her best friend needed her, so she couldn't start her work. The next day, she finally sat down and started doing research about the assignment. It turned out that she vastly underestimated the time required. The scarcity of time made her anxious, so she couldn't work as focused as she knew she could.

One day before the deadline, she still had 30% of the work left, so she quickly patched up the rest of her assignment to meet the deadline. The assignment wasn't rejected, but it wasn't a success, either.

If she had started doing the assignment on time, she could have done an outstanding job. If she dedicated the first week to it instead of the last, she could have finished it in one week as she estimated because stress and time scarcity wouldn't have invaded her brain. Also, she would have had some time to re-read and improve the work here and there if needed. But who has ever done such a thing in the history of humanity? Do something in the first week instead of the last? Very few people, my friends, very few.

Often, we know what to do, and why and how we should do it. We just haven't gotten to that unpleasant time when the pain of not doing surpasses the pain of doing. That's when we start taking action. If there is no coercive force, we sit and pass the time because it is the path of least resistance. We are natural experts in finding these paths. It's human nature. Don't judge yourself too harshly about it.

What can we do to overwrite our natural inclination towards the path of least resistance?

First, we need to become aware of what we're doing. It is natural to procrastinate on something when we are honestly fatigued, overwhelmed, or sad. For sure you won't start working on a work presentation for two months later the day after you got dumped, your dog died, or you were diagnosed with some illness. Of course you'll put off tasks of lower priority once something more meaningful arises. The procrastination I'm talking about is not of this nature.

The procrastination I'm talking about is the kind where you write about procrastination and you get such an urge to go and buy that GoPro that you'll need in Australia, yet you travel to Australia only in October (now it's August). So you leave the café heading to the mall but midway you realize what you're doing – and why – so you choose to sit down in another café, and continue your work. (I just told you the past fifteen minutes of my life from the moment I'm writing these lines.)

When you become aware that you're putting something off and you're rationalizing why, start taking action immediately. Do something small. It doesn't even have to be directly connected to the task you're delaying. Just do something that makes you happy, that you enjoy, and which makes you feel motivated. Watch a motivational video about taking action, for example.

After that, you might find it easier to start on what you need to do.

It is easier to have continuous momentum than to speed up, then come to a stop, then speed up again, then burn out. It works well in some high-intensity interval trainings, but not here. When we talk about procrastination and healthy habits, constant starts and pauses sap your energy and enthusiasm and willpower.

If you are constantly in motion, making decisions and doing things, you get into a flow state of mind. This doesn't mean you are literally in motion all day, burning your candle on both ends and suffering a heart attack at the age of 35. It means you routinely condition your mindset to take action and overcome procrastination.

Toddlers don't procrastinate. When they are hungry or thirsty, they let you know right away, sometimes quite forcefully. No waiting or procrastinating in their agenda. They start crying. They need their diaper changed right now, not tomorrow or the next month.

But then they start learning from their surroundings. About 70-75% of young people – college age to thirty – procrastinate. Of older adults, about 25-30% are still in the procrastination trap, even though they've already experienced the downside of it.

"My best friend is the one who brings out the best in me," Henry Ford stated at a reception.

Lara and Jack had been married for 12 years. They knew each other very well – knew each other's shortcomings and flaws. Lara knew that Jack was a passionate person who got fired up easily and jumped into action very quickly. However, his motivation could decrease just as quickly. She knew that if his motivation hit rock bottom, he'd probably just stop working.

She also knew that Jack could easily stay on track if he had to stop working before the most interesting task of the day. If he couldn't finish the big design, he'd be very eager to resume working the next day.

Jack knew how much trouble Lara went through to help him with his procrastinating habits. He considered himself very lucky for having such a woman by his side. After he finished each project, he found a way to show his gratitude and appreciation for her. Since Lara loved Jack's creative and unique surprises, she was almost looking forward to her husband's new projects so she could help him. They made a good team.

Why do we procrastinate?

The following list includes the main reasons people procrastinate. The first five are the most common reasons. The others are less frequently encountered; however, they round out the list to give you a more complete image.

1) **Feeling overworked.** Things start to pile up. You don't even remember which task is most important. It is difficult to prioritize when there is too much to do. In your desperation, you start working on the most urgent one. Sometimes you do things because they seem like easy fixes. This way, you deceive yourself into feeling efficient.

2) **Boring work.** Doing something you do not enjoy and don't see a way out of makes it hard to work. A task can be monotonous, tiresome, and make you sleepy. Doing the same thing day after day can get boring if you cannot find something interesting that you like about it. People working in the same job for years often can't find motivation.

3) **Fear.** Two related extremes of this feeling will lead to procrastination.

Fear of responsibility: When you stop procrastinating, you come face to face with an uncharted area of responsibility and that can scare you – for example, how many things you missed and messed up by procrastinating. Accepting responsibility for these things is a hard pill to swallow. It's easier to start procrastinating again.

Fear of taking risks: This is a major barrier to personal development. People's imagination often exaggerates possible risks. There is no action without risk, and without action, there is no meaningful life. Obstacles show the path to success.

4) **Seeking rewards.** "Why rush? It will have to get done sooner or later, but for now, it can wait." It's not like you get an award for doing it. Some people may not like to upset the status quo. People who are subject to this type of procrastination prefer to do nothing unless it is certain that there is a reward for their actions.

5) **Shame.** Shame can prevent you from asking for help when you need it.

6) **Feeling paralyzed.** If the magnitude of the task is frightening, break the problem into smaller sub-steps and execute them. These smaller, easier parts will get you moving again. How do you eat an elephant? One bite at a time.

7) **Inability to analyze.** You are unable to see the forest for the trees. In other words, you can't decipher the task because of the details. It seems too big and complicated. What are you supposed to do? What is it about? Which way should you look at it? First things first, you need to know where to start,

and then you can focus on the next step. And the next. At some point, the big picture becomes clearer.

8) **Lack of priorities.** Those who do not list their tasks – in writing – according to their importance tend to randomly jump from task to task. This can lead to chaos and inefficiency and ultimately in unachieved goals. Lack of priorities is the recipe for a downward spiral of demotivation.

9) **Forgetfulness.** You can get into the daily grind so deeply that you forget your basic tasks. That's how the brain protects itself from breaking a routine. You tend to turn on autopilot mode. If you know yourself to be forgetful it is even more important to have a calendar and a notebook where you jot down your tasks.

10) **Nervousness.** Inner tension manifests itself this way in almost everybody. There is a greater risk of making a mistake when you're nervous, and you want to avoid that. So you procrastinate. Being nervous, however, can be helpful because it mobilizes reserves, which can bring results. Finding the optimal level of it is key.

11) **Lethargy.** Sometimes people fall into self-pity. If it is a temporary condition, don't fret too much about it. We all have low points. Allow your emotions to surface and leave and get back to your life after. However, if you feel constant lethargy and think life just doesn't have meaning so you don't do anything, that's another story. If this condition is chronic you may want to talk to someone about it.

12) **Dependence.** Some people rely on others because they feel they can't do anything for themselves. They need somebody's approval or guidance. Without external control, they are like a ship without a captain, just drifting on the ocean. So they procrastinate whenever the captain is not around.

13) **Perfectionism.** Procrastination triggered by perfectionism can be caused by a fear of failure and criticism. People tense up inside, their muscles stiffen, and their brains get foggy. They want to do their jobs without mistakes, and often they delay until "the moment of perfection" because they don't feel ready. This moment may never come.

14) **Passing responsibility to others.** This person goofs and slacks off until someone else takes care of their work. They are in the background, pulling the strings until someone gets fed up and completes a large portion of their task.

15) **Fatigue.** The excuse of fatigue is one of the best "excuse" methods. There is no human on Earth who has not deferred something at least once because they were tired. As I mentioned before, sometimes this is a good excuse. But if you use it awfully often, try to look at what reason lies underneath your constant fatigue. Insufficient rest? Depression? Lack of challenge? Make sure to take care of the core problem and not use fatigue as an excuse for too long.

16) **Over-commitment.** We take on more than we can handle. We want to play on many fields at once, and this leads to complete chaos. It is hard to hold things together and figure out where to start, we tend to not do anything. This can make us seem unreliable and disorganized, even if we have the best intentions.

17) **Lack of self-discipline.** Becoming self-disciplined may be the most challenging task, especially if the consequences of lack of discipline don't show up immediately. Learning how to manage our willpower and live in a disciplined way is key to having a successful life.

18) **Distractions.** Spending hours in front of the TV or computer is a nest for procrastination. The meaningless and

empty programs, reports, and information that play on your emotions can make your life so unlived.

Six Types of Procrastination

1) The Avoider

Avoiders lack motivation to take any steps to change their situation. They are among those who give up their dreams. They don't say no because they avoid having to resist someone. They have jobs they don't like and don't find pleasure in. They are procrastinating on improving their own quality of life.

Avoiders rely on others to choose directions and make decisions for them. On one hand, this is to avoid confrontation. On the other hand, they need agreement, approval, and guidance.

2) The Perfectionist

Perfectionists think that only perfection is good enough – no big surprise here. They won't start working on a task until all the conditions are met and they have all the information they need to do the work. They document even the smallest details and collect everything they think they may need to complete an assignment.

They obsessively strive for perfection, which can be traced back to overachiever parents, a never-satisfied partner, fear of failure, and criticism. Often they tense up inside, and want to do their jobs without mistakes. They set the bar high. "What would everyone say if I don't do a perfect job?" They perceive making a mistake as shameful. Their dissatisfaction with themselves indicates a lack of self-confidence.

3) The Dreamers

Dreamers spend most of their days on autopilot mode. Often, they are so immersed in their own daydreaming that their actual life gets lost in the background. Sometimes they forget why they started what they were doing.

They can design a life so beautiful, but acting on the changes needed to make their dreams a reality hardly ever follows. Dreamers mostly know what they want, they can make good plans, but at the moment of practical implementation, their whole system comes to a halt. They stop and postpone a certain tasks until tomorrow, and engage in more "planning" instead.

When they come back to real life their mood darkens. So they escape in daydreaming again. It's a vicious cycle.

They have great potential, they just need to learn to take action. They are great planners and their challenge is to become great implementers.

4) The Pessimist

This type of person only sees the hole in a donut. When things don't go the way the Pessimist wanted, suddenly, everything becomes dark. They see resistance and rejection everywhere. Every time negative thoughts pop up, immediately replace them with reality. Question negative thoughts. Things are never as bad and hopeless as they seem in the dark. Shed some light on them intentionally.

5) The Worrier

The slightest resistance or pushback scares the Worrier. They are stopped by the first negative opinion or circumstance, and will not move until they manage to calm down, convincing themselves that it was just a false alarm. And that may take a lot of time. Then another small cloud comes, and their worrying starts all over again.

"Everything you want is on the other side of fear." – Jack Canfield

Face your fears. Accept that they exist. Get to know them. Ask:

1. What is the worst thing that can happen?
2. Write down the process and implications of this worst-case scenario as precisely as you can.
3. Prepare yourself mentally to accept it.
4. Write down every conceivable way to avoid the worst-case scenario and take action.

6) The Overachiever

The Overachiever is the person who takes on everything without thinking. They will do it all in their job and their social life, even if it's not possible. This is the person who works a lot and takes on even more – often other people's responsibilities and things get chaotic. As a result, the efficiency of their work is reduced and they get little done. They are the ultimate "multitaskers." They need to develop the ability to focus on one thing at a time.

How to overcome procrastination?

The mind is capable of achieving anything you believe in. I'm not talking about education, degrees, or academics. Napoleon Hill was among the first who stated this fundamental law, which allows all of us to achieve our goals in a comprehensible form. He stated the following:

"Whatever the mind of man can conceive and believe, it can achieve."

Regardless of how many times you've failed in the past, you can make a difference now. You always can. The key is in your hands: you must be willing to do it differently than before. You may not achieve success, but at least you'll be closer to your goal. Remember Edison and his many experiments with the lightbulb? Without him, maybe we'd still be using candles. Who knows what you could contribute to the world with resilience and grit? Maybe in 20 years, we'll sing hymns to you for being so persistent in overcoming your procrastination, taking action, and achieving something great.

Know your values, what you want, and be aware of the impact procrastination has on your life.

1. The first step is to become aware of your specific procrastination habits and decide to break the habit. Commit to this goal.
2. Step number two is to have at least one actual goal (apart from breaking procrastination). Something in deep alignment with your values, something you long for. (You know, you can exercises your goal of beating procrastination only in the context of another goal.)
3. Develop a strategy, an action plan with priorities to achieve your goal written in point b. Build a list of the tasks you can start without procrastinating on them. Small, easy steps.

4. Change your daily routines that trigger procrastination.

Charles Duhigg, the author of the book The Power of Habit, stated that each of our habits starts with a cue, some pre- action that generates the performance of the habit. For example, high tension (the cue) can lead you to overeat (the habit). Or putting on your workout clothes (the cue) triggers you to go to the gym (the habit). Habits are learned. They are not innate, thus they are changeable. Duhigg talks about a third element, closing the habit creation loop – the reward. He argues that we go through the first two steps of the habit loop, cue and the actual habit, because we're seeking a reward (consciously or subconsciously). If we are able to identify our reward, we may be able to change the habit loop around it. For example, if you overeat because you want to alleviate tension, try to find healthier coping mechanisms that will bring the same reward. Go for a run, eat healthier food, watch a short funny video… whatever it takes to get the reward but changing the habit.

On a psychological level, procrastination is a powerful emotional coping mechanism. People avoid doing something to cope with certain emotions. In a way we push the boundaries of childhood further and preserve living carefree lives, motivated by chasing the "feel-good" experience. We repeat this so often that it turns into a habit. Our self-regulation skills sometimes are like a five-year-old's: "I don't want to do it! I don't feel like it so I won't do it!"

Take action to change this habit. If I've learned anything about self-improvement, it is that only reading about it won't get me anywhere. Only taking the time to sit down and put my thoughts in written form will make the real change. Therefore, this is the best tip I can give to you, too. Sit down, take a paper and pencil, and write the following:

- Write the main goal you'd like to achieve in your life on the first page. (If you completed all the exercises thus far this should be an easy task by now.)

Nothing is mandatory. It is up to you. You made the decision that will take you out of your comfort zone. The most effective antidote for procrastination is executing an activity that requires discipline. What is discipline, in this context? Doing something even when you don't want to.

Have a to-do list.

Write down absolutely everything you need to do the next day, then prioritize the items by marking the most pressing ones URGENT. Most people who only do the urgent things during the day still become dead tired by evening.

Write down your to-do list for the next week, month, or even year, creating not just urgent but important groups. It is almost endemic that when something is not urgent, people keep postponing it. When you get to a point that something becomes urgent, you can no longer procrastinate, but by then you've created a stressful and unhealthy environment. Concentrate on the important groups, and do every important task at the proper time to save yourself the stress of "urgency."

Write a not-to-do list.

Write down anything you don't want to do or that does not need to be done. For example:

Do not waste your time in front of the television watching shows that are not useful or that you cannot learn from. You do not need to meet people who waste your time with their meaningless conversations.

Divide the larger tasks into smaller parts.

To the classic question, "How do you eat an elephant?" there is the classic answer: "One bite at a time." For example, how do you write a book? You start thinking and divide the whole thing into smaller steps. Like this:

- **Task 1** – Figure out what you want to write about. Select a topic.
- **Task 2** – Summarize the book in one sentence.
- **Task 3** – Start collecting material on the chosen topic. Explore how other people feel about the matter. Read books, watch videos, listen to podcasts, talk to strangers, and take notes.
- **Task 4** – Start outlining and writing the book.
- **Task 5** – Publish the material in printed form and/or audiobook.
- **Task 6** – Promote your product.

It is good to break the work into smaller parts, because when one part is finished, you can finally cry out, "Yeah, it's done!" and feel a little success before moving on to the next step. It is a liberating feeling. The tasks that take more than an hour can be quite energy-consuming. Their completion can take weeks, months, or a longer time. If this is the case, divide them into sub-tasks until they become manageable.

A)   Ask yourself powerful questions.

What does a good and powerful question look like? Why do we care about the answer? Now that's an excellent powerful question. Ask yourself tough, positive questions to get your brain to work on the answers. Your subconscious is the most effective partner assisting you in the battle against procrastination.

Why is ice cold? Why is the night dark? Why is the grass green? These are the questions of a small child. We grew up asking questions. We used to be good at it. By asking, we broadened our knowledge, our experience, and our emotions. Sometimes we lose this ability in our adulthood and we settle for "this is how it is" and "I don't care." That's not a growth-mindset approach. Stay curious, stay hungry. It makes a difference in life when we really understand something or someone.

B) Start your day with the "frog."

You know, that overwhelming, hard task that is much more important than the other nine combined. It is better to "eat the frog" and be done with the unpleasant tasks first. It's a relief, and makes the rest seem easy.

C) Reward yourself.

Every time you check something off your to-do list – a task completed or a section finished – reward yourself. Keep it proportional – small task, small reward; big task, big reward.

How to Find Your True Priorities?

It is not enough to know what you want. You need to understand which of these things matters the most. The best way to uncover your priorities is to get a piece of paper and write down the goals you have.

Write a maximum of five goals, dreams, or wishes. Ask questions to broaden your perspective about the importance of that particular goal. Rank the questions from 1-10 based on their importance. (10 is very important, 1 is totally meaningless.)

1. Rank the goal on a scale from 1 to 5. The first place is worth 5 points, second place is worth 4 points and so on, down to the last place with only 1 point in value. You can't give the same number twice as an answer to the question, "What is your main goal?"
2. How fulfilled would you feel if you achieved this goal? (1-10)
3. How badly would it impact you if you didn't reach this goal? (1-10)

This sounds a bit complicated, so let me illustrate the process with my own top five goals at the moment. Make sure to rank the goals as 10-9-8-7-6 even if the logical way would be 5-4-3-2-1. You'll see why later.

- Achieving my best fitness condition - ever. Writing 50 books.
- Getting to know my mother better. Finding the right partner.
- Living for three months in New Zealand.

These are my top five goals I want to reach within a given timeframe. Let's say in 2019. Now let's take them one by one:

1. Achieving my best fitness condition.
2. Ranking of importance: 7.
3. How fulfilled would you feel if you achieved this goal? 7, because fitness is my greatest outlet to challenge my body. Succeeding would make me feel proud of my physical capacity and resilience.

4. How badly would it impact you if you didn't reach this goal? 3, because even if I don't go overdo my 100 kg deadlift, the work I put in at the gym day by day wouldn't be worthless. The fact that I didn't become my all-time best this year would just push me to be better the next.
5. Writing 50 books.
6. Ranking of importance: 8.
7. How fulfilled would you feel if you achieved this goal? 8, because it would mean I really challenged my creativity and mental abilities. Furthermore, writing books is my job and passion.
8. How badly would it impact you if you didn't reach this goal? 8, for the same reasons – in negative – this goal would make me feel fulfilled if I succeeded.
9. Getting to know my mother better.
10. Ranking of importance: 9
11. How fulfilled would you feel if you achieved this goal? 10, because for 25 years, my mother was almost a stranger to me. She fell ill when I was very young, and through the years, I couldn't really detach from my messed-up childhood. I saw myself as the victim, and her the reason behind my misery. Now I can be objective about her, forgive her – and myself – and try my best to create a mother–daughter relationship.
12. How badly would it impact you if you didn't reach this goal? 9, because time is running out. She is 61 this year, and I am hardly ever home. Still, I know one can't rush emotions and acceptance, so if we just made a little progress, I would be happy.

D) Finding the right partner.

1. Ranking of importance: 10.

2. How fulfilled would you feel if you achieved this goal? 10. I know, very cheesy, but I am at that age when girls really want the next step in their life to happen.

How badly would it impact you if you didn't reach this goal? 5, because I'm not in a huge rush and I'd rather find the right person then to settle out of desperation to the first hobo just to meet the 2019 "deadline."

E) Living for three months in New Zealand.

1. Ranking of importance: 6.
2. How fulfilled would you feel if you achieved this goal? 5, because during my travels, I learned that it's not the place that matters, necessarily, but the people in it. New Zealand is the most beautiful country I've ever visited, so it definitely charged me with its raw, natural beauty. I'd be happy even if I lived in a cottage for three months, writing and living simply.
3. How badly would it impact you if you didn't reach this goal? 3. Since this is a big world and I have many goals lined up before this one, and I still have all the time in the world (hopefully) to go live in New Zealand for three months, I wouldn't be too sad.

You can add more auxiliary questions to refine your quantifiable rankings. Using only the first three parameters often brings about a tie among your goals' importance. The fourth parameter could be "How urgent is this?" if you don't have a specific deadline for the goal. Find parameters that bring relevant results. If there is a tie, you can add one more criteria that can help you resolve it.

How do you rate your own survey? Divide all your important listed goals into three groups:

1. Very important – the average of all the parameters should be eight or greater (8<X)*
2. Important – the average of all the parameters should be between six and eight (6<X<8)
3. Can wait (important, but not urgent) – the average of all the parameters is less than six (X<6)

*X is the average value of the result.

How to do the math:

1. Working with three parameters a=10 b=9 c=9

X=a+b+c=10+9+9=28/3=9.33

Thus, X=9.33

8<X=9.33

So this is a very important goal.

Let's see the ranking of my five goals:

- Fitness goal: 7+7+4= 18/3 = 6 – Important
- Writing 50 books: 8+8+8= 24/3 = 8 – Very important
  Getting to know my mother better: 9+10+9= 28/3 = 9.3 – Very important
- Finding the right partner: 10+10+5 = 25/3 = 8.3 – Very important
- Living for three months in New Zealand: 6+5+3 =14/3 = 4.6 – Can wait

As you can see, based on my calculations, there is a little change of order in the de facto importance of my goals, compared to how I ranked them initially. If I only answered just one question, namely the ranking of importance, the order would be this: relationship – mother – books – fitness – New Zealand. But using and ranking auxiliary questions, it turns out, fixing the relationship with my mother should be my most important priority. If I had more auxiliary questions, my real ranking of importance would have become even more accurate.

As you can see, thinking slowly about your goals can lead you to more real and accurate answers than to listen to your snap judgment.

2. PRODUCTIVITY

The Oxford Dictionary defines productivity this way: noun. The rate at which a worker, a company or a country produces goods, and the amount produced, compared with how much time, work and money is needed to produce them.

How would you define productivity?

We often say things like: "I should be more productive," or "You should increase your productivity." What do you think when you hear these remarks? That you should be quicker with your work? That you should produce more in the same amount of time? That you should generate more money?

Whatever it means to you, one thing is certain – the more productive you are, whatever your reasons, the better. So how do you maximize your productivity? We'll explore it in this chapter.

IT'S About Time

YOU MAY WONDER how some people always finish their work on time, even when they have a heavier workload than others. I'm sure each and every one of us has a friend, coworker, or acquaintance who is always on time and delivers high-quality work. If you don't know somebody like this, then you're probably this person.

Efficient people have one thing in common: a superpower called mastering the use of their time. Everyone has 24 hours at their disposal. Some actually use most of these efficiently.

And yes, sleeping is an efficient way to use your time too. Without the right amount of sleep, it is impossible to maintain focus for long. You'd be in Zombieland all day if it weren't for Nescafé, Red Bull, and other caffeine distributors whose profit margins grow as a result of your struggle to get "into the zone." So by not sleeping enough, you increase someone's macroeconomic productivity – but not yours.

There are times when you're not in the mood to do anything. I often fall prey to a wave of disinterest like when Bruno Mars sings, "Today, I don't feel like doing anything," in "The Lazy Song." It is completely normal to feel unmotivated. You can't burn with the brightest flame all the time. Eventually, you'll feel like you don't want to do anything, and there's nothing wrong with that.

But there is always something to do. Even when you're unmotivated, there are "must-do" activities. Just as we saw in the chapter on procrastination, there are lots of boring tasks we put off because they are tiresome, and it does not help our sense of productivity. We can still do stuff like going to the post office, paying bills, going grocery shopping, answering emails, etc.

You may say you are not interested or thrilled about anything. Well, that's the perfect time to do the boring things. When you are not excited about anything else, you won't feel you are wasting your precious "in-the-zone" time on unproductive and dull tasks.

And as counterintuitive as it may sound, doing unproductive things in an unproductive mood actually increases your productivity. When you overcome your boredom, you're able to focus 100% on the things that move you forward without being distracted with the "chores."

If you make the effort to tackle these boring tasks instead of doing nothing during your unmotivated time, you'll realize you are actually doing something. You're not on an award-winning mission, but something is better than nothing. And this will give you a sense of satisfaction, the feeling of a day well spent, and the kick you need to be in a more creative, motivated, and productive mood later.

THE BENEFITS of Getting Disconnected

IN THE DIGITAL WORLD, productivity is exposed to more distractions than ever. We have the Internet with its infinite rabbit hole of information, social media, and games.

The best advice on how to avoid distractions comes from Derek Sivers, founder of CD Baby and author of Anything You Want. He states that the best and most productive time of his life was when he totally disconnected. Mr. Sivers experienced the power of disconnection when he was 22 years old and spent five months alone in a house in Oregon. In his book, he writes: "In those five months, I wrote and recorded over 50 songs, made huge improvements in my instrumental skills, read 20 books (some of which changed my life), lost 20 pounds, and got into the best physical shape of my life."

His next solitary adventure resulted in the creation of CD Baby, which became a 22-million-dollar company.

Mr. Sivers claims the reason he enjoys solitude isn't because he dislikes people; on the contrary, he says his best ideas come from his mind when it is in a state of flow, when he unleashes his creativity and excludes all the noises, news, emails, pings, and meetings.

His ultimate advice for people seeking success is to disconnect. He writes, "Even if just for a few hours. Unplug. Turn off your phone and Wi-Fi. Focus. Write. Practice. Create. That's what's rare and valuable these days."

You may think that you don't have the time to disconnect. Tony Robbins says, "If you don't have ten minutes for yourself, you don't have a life." Yes, sometimes even 10, 20 minutes of disconnection can make a significant difference. Turn on your internal focus, listen to your thoughts, and find out why you have those specific thoughts in that moment.

Live a little bit of "you" time, then go back to work. If you can afford a few hours a day or week, let's say after work or on the weekend, even better. If you are bold or free enough, give disconnection a try for a week or a month. Even four days can make a huge difference. In the next pages, I will tell you why and how.

BE in the Moment

A FEW YEARS AGO, I felt overwhelmed with work. In the last one and a half years, I've written books constantly, without rest. I've read more than sixty books, I have coached people, done my own book marketing, designs, everything. So I went for a five-week holiday. I would like to emphasize the word "holiday." I travel almost all the time, but it is never a holiday. I work, and coach just the same way, only I ask for my coffee in a different language. This was a holiday. Still, my first, most memorable break lasted only four days. In mid-August 2016, I felt like I needed a rest – just a short one.

I quickly booked a log cabin in the Romanian mountains for four days. It was located in a national reserve in an isolated village of 343 people. All I wanted was silence, peace, and no Internet. I wanted to meditate, sleep, and do nothing exciting or busy, no people, no nothing. You can imagine what it was like.

I'll never forget that trip. It opened my eyes to the fact that what you want is not always what you need. Initially, I went there to chill and be alone, but instead I met a man (the owner) who was an ex-pop star in Romania and wanted to live a more peaceful life. He spends six months every summer in Romania, in that little village of 343 people, and tries to help the community. In the winter, he teaches people to surf in Uruguay. What a life, I thought.

I wanted peace, but I needed noise. I needed that inspiring person in my life to remind me that there's nothing on that mountaintop I'm trying to reach with my relentless work. He was there, he saw it, he felt alone, and now he just longs for the journey on that mountain, and to help other climbers with directions. He impressed me. I think he is truly free, but then, who knows?

Freedom is a subjective state of mind. Maybe his life of freedom would be a prison of unpredictability for someone else. I went there to be alone and reflect on my life, to be in the moment, to eat simple food, enjoy the sunshine and listen to the bugs. I wanted to be free – free from my mind and my troubles.

I felt then that I wasn't capturing anything at the moment, but actually, I did. I didn't realize it at that time, but today, I feel everything that my senses couldn't embrace back then. The memory feels wonderful.

During this four-day trip I also managed to push through one of my fears. Have you ever feared something, and then the next moment, found you loved that fear because it excited you, and it changed your opinion about yourself completely? This was paragliding for me.

While discovering the mountains, I saw some people paragliding, and there, in that moment, after thinking for only five minutes, I decided I wanted to do it. A blink. There were many first times: the first time I didn't have to consider the price; the first time I didn't hesitate and analyze every detail; the first time I didn't listen to the voice of fear in my head. I was there, in the moment. Now I realize I was 100% aware that if something went wrong up there, I'd die, and I was totally okay with it. If I could choose how to die, it would probably be by falling out of the sky toward a beautiful landscape below. It was true freedom; when I ran downhill with the expert, my legs didn't shake. I just felt now, now, now was the moment, and in the next one, I was in the sky, my legs and arms flying in the sky. I screamed, I screamed as loud as I could, and it was so liberating!

All that journey, I was in the moment, but I didn't realize I was in the moment until later. Maybe people are in the moment more often than they realize. Maybe by focusing so much on the moment, we actually take away from the moment. I can feel so much now. And I felt so little then. Maybe the power of memorable happiness is stronger than momentary happiness.

One thing is clear: since that journey, I got back my spirit, my desire to work, to create, to help. Not myself, initially, but others. That trip inspired me to start travelling. If I only work, I can do it anywhere in the world, I thought. But at least I meet new people, I get new impressions, I can understand how this awesome world works. I don't regret living on the road – for three years now – even though sometimes it has its dark sides. I can't see my family, I lost connection with my friends, I've experienced jetlag, had to get to understand a new city, discover the best location to live, and was even bitten by a monkey (no kidding). All in all, it is still a wonderful state of living, and I'm eternally grateful for it.

- The productivity lessons I harvested from the cottage visit and my travels are:
- An occasional change of scenery can help you escape the inevitable boredom of (even useful) daily routines.
- What you want and expect is not always what you need. "Life is like a box of chocolates; you never know what you're gonna get." – Forrest Gump. So be open to the possibilities and say yes to unexpected, but exciting things.
- If you focus too intently on being in the moment, you might lose it. Being in the moment is not about consciously knowing yes, I'm in the moment, but about enjoying everything around us. It's best if you're not aware that you're in the moment. It means you are actively in it and not just thinking about it.
- Every person we meet can teach us something. By meeting new people, we get perspectives on how others live and can evaluate whether we're lucky with our lives and get a boost to do things wholeheartedly, or whether we should find better options for ourselves.
- A counterintuitive lesson: skipping a few days of focusing on productivity will enhance your long-term productivity.

OPTIMIZE YOUR WORK

REGARDLESS OF WHETHER you're self-employed or you have a regular job, you need consistency. This consistency should reflect in your daily habits. Good productivity habits are predictable.

In other words, to minimize your lost time, you need to know exactly what you want to do, when you want to do it, and approximately how much time will it take. This is one way people make the most of their time. They minimize time wasted between tasks.

You may think 15 minutes is not much time, but if you waste this amount of time eight times a day, that's two hours. If you sleep eight hours a night, it means you have 16 active hours. Two hours is too much time to be wasted thinking about what to do next. Imagine how many things you can do in two hours. If you have a clear schedule for each day (including weekends), you instantly gain 14 hours a week, which is almost another full day's active time.

Having a clear schedule is helpful for developing a routine. I have a very clear schedule, and it helps my life enormously. I have a big picture of what I want to do in the next year (how many books I want to write, how many books I want to read, which books, how many hours I can coach, etc.). I also have a monthly plan. Every Sunday, I place a Post-It note on each day of the next week with four tasks for each day. These are work-related tasks only; they do not include chores like cooking and washing the dishes.

But since I mentioned it, work optimization includes minimizing the time wasted on other, non-work-related routines – like household tasks and other obligations. First, decide how much time you are willing to sacrifice for these tasks, then stick to it. But don't forget the opportunity cost each task involves. For example, if you don't want to spend time cooking, you can order food or eat out. The benefit is that you save the cooking and dishwashing time. Usually, it is more expensive to eat out, and if the place you choose to eat is busy, you may save only a couple of minutes.

If you don't mind cooking, but you hate going grocery shopping, there's a solution for you. There are many fresh food home delivery services that mail you all the ingredients and recipes for three to five meals for two to four people a week. It doesn't sound cheap, but the price per meal per person is usually not more than $8-$10. Because all the ingredients are fresh and more special than rice and chicken, I'd say it's a good deal. You can prepare most meals in about 40 minutes, and they are delicious.

You can optimize your work by defining your workplace. If you work in an office, it's easier, but even if you work at home or are a "digital nomad," you should be able to establish a place to work. Don't make it anything fancy. What I say is exactly what I mean: a place where you work and do nothing else. There should be no TV or other distractions. Make sure this place is comfortable, quiet, and has enough lights and clean air.

SMALL TRICKS TO Set You on Track

OH, those mornings… when you'd only like to sleep just 10 more minutes. Yes, I agree, there are few more demoralizing things than waking up early on demand. There's a big difference between this and when you don't have to wake up early, but you choose to. Waking up early by choice fills your heart with self-appreciation, pride, and a sense of accomplishment. You are awake, it's early, and you have so many chances to make the most of your day!

Why is it so horrible to wake up when you have to go to work, then? Who knows? Maybe the fact that it is compulsory, that you do it because you're afraid of getting fired or scolded by your boss. Or maybe you do it simply because you hate where you have to go after you wake up.

There are some good morning routines that can help make your mornings more motivated and productive.

- Put your alarm as far from your bed as possible. This is how I make sure to never wake up late or fall back to sleep. If your alarm is out of reach, you'll have to get up, walk to wherever you left it, and make it shut up. Finally! Phew. That was loud, you think. You blink twice, and slowly but surely, your engines start working.

- Eat a quick breakfast. There are so many nutritional theories – how much you should eat, when you should eat, etc. And almost all of them contradict each other. So I'll share with you what I do, because this is the experience I trust enough to dispense: I love to eat more in the morning, but not too much. Years ago, I read an article about eating more protein in the morning, and I tried it. It proved to be true, so I'm recommending it to you. It certainly works for me and for many other people, but we don't all function the same way, so don't take my advice as gospel. Consider trying it, and if you find it beneficial, stick with it.

I USUALLY EAT the following things in the morning: a protein shake (I shake it with an Americano coffee so I can also get my caffeine dose), a protein bar (20 g protein, preferably low- carb), scrambled eggs with only two yolks out of the three eggs, or oats mixed with cottage cheese and some cinnamon and honey for flavor. All these foods keep me full until lunchtime, and all of them are kickass energy boosters.

- Try to tailor-make your work time. We are different, not only in our breakfast needs, but also regarding when we are the most productive. More and more workplaces are starting to recognize this, and some are really putting the emphasis on quality of work instead of the quantity of hours their employees spend in the office. Some offices are open to negotiating special work schedules. You never know until you ask.

GO TO YOUR MANAGER, boss, or whoever you report to. Some companies can't afford a raise in salaries, but if you are a good worker, instead of a raise they might be inclined to change your 9-5 shift to 10-6, 11-7, or 7-3.

- Create your ideal work environment. This can include decorations, adding or reducing light, increasing or decreasing the number of colleagues around you, and so on. You want to be as focused as possible; you want to make the most of your knowledge. Learn to ask for what you need. If your requests are reasonable and your company is growth-oriented, I'm sure they'll take some measures to assure the best possible environment for their workforce.

DON'T BE afraid or ashamed to say no. If you are in the middle of a project, a thought, or simply your relaxation time, tell your colleagues, kindly but firmly, that you need some alone time. It's not easy, at first. You may fear they'll get upset with you, but if you respect their privacy and you are normally friendly and approachable, people will respect you even more for your strong sense of self-respect.

- Don't forget to exercise. I know, it sounds awful, especially if you cast your vote against it a long time ago. Whether you like it or not, doing physical activity is part of a healthy daily routine. Don't do something you absolutely hate, but don't put your hand on your heart and swear to yourself that you're not interested in anything.

IS THERE something that if you had time, money, energy, etc., you'd gladly try? Identify what type of sport it is: competitive, team, high-intensity, low-intensity, monotonic, changeable, or something you can do at home. If you really don't have the chance to do something you'd like, try to find something similar but affordable in time, energy, and money. Be creative today YouTube is a talking encyclopedia, and eBay is the fairy godmother who can make your wish come true quite cheaply. I'm sure you can figure out how, what, and when to work out.

- Improve your sleeping habits. The first thing I was willing to pay money for was bed-related stuff. I have weird expectations for where I sleep – like the pillow must be memory foam, not too soft, not too hard; no polyester quilts; and if I drop a quarter on my sheet, it should bounce. Also, I need quiet and darkness. It's crazy, yes, but I know I can have a restful night's sleep if all these conditions are met. And, at least when I am at home, I like to have them.

IF YOU FEEL that anything on your bed distracts you from sleep because it's uncomfortable – change it. It's a good investment. Learn what physical conditions you must have to get a good night's sleep and create them. Sometimes these changes can have a placebo effect too, like when you buy a new dress and wear it for the first time and feel much prettier in that dress than you did in your old one.

IF YOUR SLEEPING problems are not physical, but related to mental issues, depending on the problem you can try to change your daily routines, or in severe cases, go to a doctor or ask for professional advice. Caffeine, eating, or sitting in intense light until bedtime can, for example, increase the chance of insomnia or shallow sleeping. Also, if you eat a big meal before bed, your brain will stay active while digesting, so sleeping can be challenging.

DR. NITUN VERMA, the medical director of the Washington Township Center for Sleep Disorders in Freemont, California, has some solutions. She says we have to give our brain the "farming environment," meaning we have to stay in the dark during the night and light during the day.2 He advises people to start dimming lights a few hours before we plan to sleep. There are some excellent lights on the market with adjustable intensity that can be a good long-term investment. It's interesting that darkness and light affects blind people's sleep too. Dr. Verma says that even if they can't see, light still stimulates nerves in the eyeball.

A LAST PIECE of sleep-related advice: Have a go-to-sleep as well as a wake-up alarm. It is more difficult to respect the bedtime than the wake-up alarm, but strengthen your resolve and include this small change in your daily routine. If you know that you'll still waste time with this and that, set a warning alarm 30 minutes before the actual bedtime alarm and another one five minutes before. After the second alarm, put down whatever you are doing, brush your teeth, and go to bed.

- Get out in nature. We are part of nature, but in the rush of daily life, we tend to overlook this important fact. Research has proven that walking in a forest or on a shore, taking a nap in a hammock in a park, or simply enjoying the birds' singing can significantly reduce stress and improve creative thinking and memory. A study conducted by the Dutch National Survey of General Practice concluded that people who live in a 1–3 km (0.6–1.8 miles) radius of a green area had less stress and perceived or actual health problems.

ANOTHER STUDY CONDUCTED by Robert Ulrich at Texas A&M University proves that adding flowers or green plants to your office increases creativity significantly. This study lasted for eight months and resulted in a 15% increase in ideas from male workers, and more flexible, problem-solving skills with female employees.

TIPS From The Tip of the Mountain

EVERYBODY DOES IT DIFFERENTLY. As long as you make some changes to improve your daily routines and build better habits, it doesn't matter which tips from this book you choose to implement. I try to show you as many options as possible so you can choose the ones that are the most fitting, helpful, and relevant to you. You are seven billion; I am one. It is very hard to find solutions that can work for everyone, so I've decided to give many options from different perspectives to give you a greater chance of finding something valuable and applicable.

I read a lot. Often, I read a great book that goes in-depth on one topic or solution. Most of the time, I find these in-depth explanations to be interesting and thoughtful, but I can hardly ever apply them to my life. However, when I read a book that has a main topic and presents a variety of solutions, I can pick which ones I know will fit my life and then search out a more in-depth book on that particular topic.

So, in the following pages, I'll present you with some tactics that world-famous people use to make their daily routines better.

1. Jack Dorsey

THE CEO of Square and co-founder of Twitter is a busy guy. He has two huge companies to oversee, and decided to work eight hours a day, Monday to Friday, on each one. Yes, that's 16 hours a day, five days a week. When I grow up, I don't think I want to be Jack Dorsey.

BEFORE WE START FUNDRAISING and donating our free hours to Mr. Dorsey, I'd like to add that he worked these intense hours for only a limited time, and right now he is more focused on Square. But how did he manage to keep it together when he was working 16-hour days?

HE THEMED HIS DAYS. He developed a strict structure of daily and weekly routines for both his companies and followed this structure with steadfast discipline. Every weekday, he spent time on one particular area or aspect of his businesses. On Mondays, he worked on management, on Tuesdays, he focused on products, and so on.

IF YOU FEEL your schedule is tight, especially if you're an entrepreneur, you could try this system. It gives you a structured and predictable weekly routine and lifts the weight of decision fatigue from your shoulders. There will always be distractions and interruptions in your daily theme, but be prepared and don't lose track of the essential task of the day, and when the distraction goes away, be ready to continue where you left off.

2. Tim Ferriss

WE COULD SAY that Tim Ferriss, the author of The 4-Hour Workweek, is the opposite of the Jack Dorsey and his 16-hour workdays. If you read his book, you'll know that Mr. Ferriss' life wasn't always as easy as a four-hour workweek would sound – quite the contrary. But with resourcefulness and a lot of hard work, he developed systems for himself that allowed him to have more free time and a relaxed lifestyle.

SO WHAT ADVICE does he have on daily routines and habits? Nothing. Why? Because he doesn't have one. His routine is to not have a routine, and to keep everything flexible. His daily routine is never the same – he does what he wants on any particular day. He has, however, some ground rules, like no phone calls or appointments on Fridays and Mondays, so he can have long weekends whenever he wants. He doesn't have extravagant programs and systems, but he does cherish his freedom of choice, and so he does most of his work in minimal time, thereby maximizing his output.

3. Evan Williams

JUST FOR THE sake of finding middle ground between Jack Dorsey and Tim Ferriss, I present the daily routine of Evan Williams, co-founder of Twitter, Blogger, and Medium.

HE LEAVES his office midday every day to visit the gym. I mentioned previously that we are not the same when it comes to productivity or our most active hours. Mr. Williams realized it's not very productive for him to be at the gym in the morning. He found he is more productive at work in the morning, but loses focus in the middle of the day. So he decided to go to the office early and take a two-hour midday break to go to the gym. He gets refreshed at the gym and also breaks the monotony so when he returns to the office, he can concentrate with a fresh mind again.

IF YOU CAN SWING IT, try taking a midday break to do something totally different – train, exercise, or do something else that gives you pleasure. Return to working one or two hours later and you'll feel the difference.

3.   PHILOSOPHY

When we think about changing daily routines and habits, we usually think about certain actions, but our actions are the result of our thoughts. These thoughts elicit feelings and emotions, and based on these emotions, we take actions. This is called the TEA model: thoughts, emotions, and actions. Let's add a fourth element; this element is the result of the previous three.

DOES this make TEA model the TEAR model? Let's hope they are tears of joy, not sadness. All jokes aside, if we want to understand what is currently happening in our lives and where our results come from, the equation would be: thoughts + emotions + actions = results.

ACCORDING TO NEURO-LINGUISTIC PROGRAMMING (NLP), the

thoughts that elicit our emotions are "sponsoring thoughts" in opposition to conscious thoughts that make up the context of the way we perceive the world.1 Everything else in our internal landscape, our conscious thoughts, our emotions, our beliefs, come from profound contexts that we view the world through. If we change the context, not only will the thoughts change, but so will the emotions and abilities we have inside us.

IT IS important to have guiding principles for your life. Some people don't; they just fly around following the current "trends." They change their behavior and values as the trends change. Without more lasting guiding principles – a life philosophy if you like – it is difficult to determine life goals. Without goals, it is almost impossible to build routines that lead you to a better life. Even if one has a vague inclination toward something they consider a goal, if it is not rooted in a deep belief, its execution will run short on motivation and willpower.

What do you believe in? Do you know your life philosophy? What do you base your life decisions on? Why? What new habits could help you live by your highest standards?

If you look at the other side of the coin, you could say that if you lack life goals, you also lack a clear philosophy in life. That's right, it works the other way around as well. If people don't have certain expectations from life, and they're not aware of what values they cherish, they'll float on the wind like an empty plastic bag. When they are on their deathbed, looking back they realize how much time was wasted. They didn't go for something that would have been valuable; instead, they wasted time because you let distractions dominate their life.

Whatever life philosophy you embrace, your life will be better than if you tried to live without one. Don't think about anything complicated here. It's not like you have to read all the works from great thinkers, or that you must adopt one philosophy 100%. Just have a clear vision of life's guiding principles and values that are the most meaningful to you.

In the following chapter, I will present you with different life principles and values gathered from my readings. They can all lead you to a successful life. Based on your core values, you can consider adopting some of them.

FOR THOSE WHO value hard work over passion.

I RECENTLY RE-READ Cal Newport's book So Good They Can't Ignore You about how to become successful in your job and how to create the life you want. His advice is almost the opposite of what we usually hear. Most of the time, we hear advice on how to follow our passion, to leave our jobs, and to

stop the grind and create ourselves.2 Well, Mr. Newport thinks differently, and this doesn't mean he is wrong. Moreover, his thoughts are worth reading for everybody who has a passion-oriented life philosophy (I'm one of those people). It's always good to know the alternatives to our beliefs, as well as the thoughts that challenge our beliefs.

REGARDING YOUR CAREER, the path to a good life is more complex than simply asking yourself:

WHAT SHOULD I do with my life?

FOLLOWING your passion may not be the best advice out there when you think about creating the career of your dreams. According to Mr. Newport, the "follow your passion" conventional wisdom is wrong. The passion-oriented career philosophy not only fails to describe how exactly people can end up working their dream jobs, but also, for most people, it can actually make life worse by leading them to a frequent job-shifting lifestyle, as well as lower income. Not to mention the high levels of anxiety indecision and the paradox of choice creates.

NOW, you may think, if following your passion is not good advice, what should you do?

PASSION HAS no direct impact on creating a fulfilling work life in the long run. Even the most exciting, creative, and diverse jobs, like being a writer, gets dull and repetitive after a while. Trust me, I know. If you base your choice solely on passion, that flame will burn out quicker than your Ikea candles.

STOP FOCUSING on finding the right work. Instead, focus on working right, and gradually learn to love what you do. Cal Newport states that the more years you spend doing your job and the better you become at it (due to experience and diligence), the more you'll consider it a calling. The more experience, expertise, and praise you receive, the more you'll grow to love what you do. The longer you stick with something and the better you become at it, the more passionate you'll feel about it. We, humans, are such creatures – we love to feel special, good, admired, we like to excel. Even naturally talented people can attest that not their talent (which drove their passion initially) granted them excellence but the repetitive, chore-like hard work they invested in their talent. People who rely solely on their talent are… well, we don't know who they are because they never raise above a certain level.

YOU MAY NOW THINK, "But I'm not talented in anything, what should I do? Does hard work help me too?" Sure it does. Remember that you're in competition with yourself first and foremost. You can level up your skills in a life area and become the best version of yourself. You may never become the best in your entire industry in the world. If you have such aspirations, you need talent, luck, and a bunch of other factors and you still may never get where you want. I don't know what the recipe is to become the best in the world because I'm not the best in the world in anything. (Even in a video game called Mortal Kombat

X I only succeeded to rank 4th on the international leaderboard for like thirty minutes, which is the greatest world-scale accomplishment I ever achieved.) But I'm good at building a life that I enjoy living. That's my goal. If your goal is something similar, keep reading.

I WISH to give you a coherent, step-by-step guide through Mr. Newport's philosophy so you can embrace it easily. My summary doesn't replace reading the actual book so if you're feeling by any way touched by it, go ahead and read it.

THE PATH TO THE "CRAFTSMAN MINDSET."

WHAT WE FIRST LEARN FROM Cal Newport is that "follow your passion" is awful career advice. In the book he refers to this idea as "the passion hypothesis." He argues that instead of getting sold for the passion hypothesis, one should invest resources into adopting the "craftsman mindset." By craftsman mindset Newport means focusing on developing rare and valuable skills, as they will lead to distinguished career outcomes. He adds that autonomy is the most important aspect of a "perfect" job. When debating between two jobs, Newport urges to choose the one with higher autonomy over the one with lower autonomy.

Feeling that your job has a "higher purpose" or that you're on a "mission" adds a lot of value to your day-to-day relationship with what you do for a living.

THE PASSION HYPOTHESIS EXPLAINED.

REALISTS MIGHT CONDESCENDINGLY smile at the idea of "just follow your passion or die trying" as being naïve but Newport takes the argument one step further and says that the passion hypothesis is not only a naïve wish, it can be dangerous one. In the book he presents a 2010 Conference Board survey of U.S. job satisfaction:

"[…] found that only 45 percent of Americans describe themselves as satisfied with their jobs. This number has been steadily decreasing from the mark of 61 percent recorded in 1987, the first year of the survey. As Lynn Franco, the director of the Board's Consumer Research Center notes, this is not just about a bad business cycle: 'Through both economic boom and bust during the past two decades, our job satisfaction numbers have shown a consistent downward trend.

Based on the data, the passion hypothesis has a direct correlation with the decline in job satisfaction. When people adopt the passion hypothesis, their expectations go berserk, they become convinced that there's a magical job waiting for them out there somewhere, and when they find it, their lives will instantly become meaningful. Such a job simply doesn't exist. And if these people put their odds of life meaning into finding such a workplace, they will constantly be job-hopping, feeling like they don't measure up. Eventually, they will think that something's inherently wrong with them for not finding this nonexistent job.

The other reason why the passion hypothesis is skewed is because clearly defined passion is really rare. The Canadian psychologist Robert J. Vallerand led a research team in 2002 and they surveyed 539 Canadian university students to find out how many of them had career-related passions. It turned out that the majority of them had hobby-related passions. It's hard to follow a passion you don't have, in this case a career passion, Newport argued, who found the results representative.

Amy Wrzesniewski, a professor at Yale School of Management, participated in a study of college administrative assistants. The interesting answer they found in this study was that the greatest predictor of an assistant considering work as a calling was the number of years spent on the job. Put simply, the more experienced the assistant was, the more likely it was they enjoyed and felt passionate about their job.

In order to get something worthy and valuable, you have to give something worthy and valuable in exchange – this is the experience and rare expertise you develop over years of working. To be considered great at your work does not just require courage, but also skill. Mr. Newport calls this the "Self-Determination Theory."

In Mr. Newport's analysis, hard work and excellence come first and that may be followed by passion. You might wonder how you will find the motivation to stick with what you do if you hate doing it. His book answers this question. Scientists figured that instead of finding a way of "matching work to pre- existing ability, interests, passions, or personality," you should motivate yourself by taking the following three psychological needs into consideration:

- Autonomy: having control over your day, feeling that your work matters.
- Competence: feeling good at what you do.
- Relatedness: feeling connected to people around you.

THE ASSISTANTS in Wrzesniewski's study enjoyed their jobs because their increased competence translated to increased autonomy. "When you become better at what you do, not only do you get the sense of accomplishment that comes from being good, but you're typically also rewarded with more control over your responsibilities."

Like all good things in life, it takes time to increase competence and earn the autonomy needed to create fulfillment.

THE CRAFTSMAN MINDSET

Good things stem from mastery, Newport concludes, and argues that instead of the passion hypothesis we should adopt what he calls the craftsman mindset. He basically means looking at your job as a craft: gain "rare and valuable skills" until you're "so good they can't ignore you."

NEWPORT BRINGS to the table "The Career Capital Theory of Great Work" to substantiate his argument.

- Great work has rare and valuable traits. Jobs we are dreaming of are essentially creative, allowing self-expression, creating an impact, and giving control over to one's hand to balance work and life.

- To get such a job, one needs to offer rare and valuable skills in return. Newport calls these rare and valuable skills "career capital."
- The craftsman mindset, by its essence, is the pursuit of acquiring rare and valuable skills.

BUT AS WITH ANY RULE, Mr. Newport's thesis has certain exceptions. There are times you shouldn't apply the "craftsman mindset," as he calls his alternative to the passion mindset. These exceptions are in the following cases:

- When the job you do has few or no opportunities to distinguish yourself with relevant skills;
- When the job is in opposition to your core values, or you think about it as useless, or even harmful; or
- You have to share your work with people you don't like and can't relate to.

AVOID CONTROL TRAPS

"Okay, I understand, I need to master rare and valuable skills, but what is an ideal job for that?" you may ask. Great question.

Autonomy plays a big role in job satisfaction. "The more control you have in your job, the more likely you are to stay and enjoy doing it," Newport says. But remember, control craves capital. If you are not "good enough" in your job, you may not get the autonomy you seek – yet. You can't demand better treatment without putting something of value on the proverbial table first. There's another caveat in the story. If the control you're seeking only benefits you, your employers won't be so willing to give it to you – even if you have enough career capital. Why? Because everybody wants to harness benefits for themselves.

Thus it's important to keep in mind that even when you have the rare and valuable skills and you're bargaining for more control, you'll hit some resistance.

"When deciding whether to follow an appealing pursuit that will introduce more control into your work life, seek evidence of whether people are willing to pay for it. If you find this evidence, continue. If not, move on," Newport quotes of Derek Sivers in his book. In other words, make sure that people would be willing to pay for your expertise. If you can be sure of that, it means that you tapped into a rare and valuable skill.

I wanted to present Cal Newport's philosophy because it offers a great alternative to the conventional "follow your passion" mindset. Trying to look at your career from this perspective can be difficult in the beginning, but long term, it can bring you satisfaction.

Depending on what your main value is, if having peace of mind is more important than seeking adventure, adopting Cal Newport's philosophy can help you create better daily "action" routines.

THE STOIC WAY of Living a Good Life

WHAT IS the core value of your life? I really hope that you thought about it by this point.

The stoic's core value is this: you're unlikely to have a happy and meaningful life if you don't overcome your insatiability. And when it comes to happiness, according to the stoics, you'll be the happiest when you learn to find joy in what you have and in what comes from within.

Our unhappiness is rooted in our insatiable nature. We want to become happy due to something external – let's say a promotion, or buying a new car. We start working hard to achieve this goal, but when we get it, we instantly lose interest. We want something else instead, something even bigger. This doesn't mean that we shouldn't want more, or that we shouldn't strive to become better, but it means we need to learn how to simultaneously appreciate what we have and pursue future goals that bring meaning in our life.

The easiest way to achieve happiness is to want the things you already have.

In A Guide to the Good Life: The Ancient Art of Stoic Joy, William Irvine describes the most important values stoicism teaches us. Following Cato, Seneca, and Marcus Aurelius' work, Mr. Irvine created a great and easy-to-follow book about stoicism. For the sake of completeness, I recommend you read his book. If you are more interested in stoicism, read the aforementioned ancient geniuses' works also. There's a lot in these books when it comes to following a life-changing philosophy.

One of the core values of stoic philosophy is self-discipline. Having relative control over your thoughts, and thus your actions, you can walk towards your life goals more deliberately and predictably. With a lack of self-discipline, you have to walk a path determined by someone else.

Tranquility is another state highly praised by the stoics. It is a psychological state in which people experience negative emotions like grief, anxiety, and fear, but also positive emotions, like joy. Experiencing any and every emotion is perfectly human and fine.

According to Seneca, you have to learn to use your reasoning ability to get rid of all that intrigues or scares you. Accept that the world is bipolar – good and bad coexist. If you expect only good, your life will be stressful and sad. Thus if you compulsively reject negative emotions, events just perpetuate your afflictions. The more you learn to accept, sit with, and let go every emotion and not get attached to them, the more tranquility and freedom you'll have in your life.

It is often part of our daily routine to take what we have for granted – our job, our well-equipped kitchen, our bank account, even the air we breathe and the health we have. Stoics encourage us to change this daily routine by thinking about and practicing poverty. They encourage us to start thinking about losing everything we take for granted – our health, including our ability to speak, walk, swallow; our family; wealth; or freedom. How would you feel if you lost your ability to speak, hear, walk, breathe, and swallow? How would you feel if you lost your freedom?

This is not negative thinking, but a practical way to enhance the feelings of gratitude toward what we own. The greatest values in life are often what we don't even think about, and do very little to cherish them. Instead, we chase empty, valueless objects and objectives.

If you allow only pleasure and comfort in your life, nothing will seem bearable when a crisis comes. This is not because that crisis is too much to bear, but because you became soft. Make sure you don't get too comfortable. This way, you'll be able to appreciate comfort better and be happier when you get it.

If you expose yourself to self-chosen discomfort from time to time, you'll be more able to handle hard times that bring true discomfort. You could also say that you'll have a larger comfort zone in regard to unpredictable events.

Exposing yourself to discomfort includes dealing with annoying people. When someone's behavior upsets you, reflect for a few minutes on your own shortcomings. By doing this, you will become more empathetic to others and realize that often, what you find annoying about others may be something you do also. What upsets people is not the facts themselves, but their judgments on these facts. Also, refusing to respond to an insult is one of the most effective reactions.

A stoic philosophy seems to be difficult to adopt in our money, fame, and pleasure-focused world. However, if you learn to simplify your life just a little based on these ancient wisdoms, you'll become much happier. As a daily habit, introduce days of low modern stimuli.

FOR EXAMPLE, decide that every Saturday you'll disconnect from the world, and that you'll try to live as people lived before television, Internet, or telephones were invented. You can also practice poverty; have a set of very cheap and low-quality clothes and consciously wear them one day a month while you eat cheap food and only drink water. Try going out in the rain without an umbrella or raincoat. Learn to value the things you have. And to be able to truly value them, you have to experience what it would be like to lose them.

4. FOCUS

Do you ever find yourself losing focus? One night, I was at a work dinner and my mind kept wandering. I had a bunch of things I needed to get done that night, and I simply couldn't focus on what was being said by all of my coworkers. Obviously, this wasn't the best situation to put myself in. As much as I tried to focus, their voices were like the teachers from Charlie Brown. All I heard was mumbling and noise, with zero comprehension lasting in my mind. One of my coworkers stopped mid-story and asked, "Are you listening?" Immediately feeling like a student being caught by a teacher, I exclaimed, "Yes! Please, continue," before drinking a whole glass of water and nodding when I was supposed to during the tale. All of us felt awkward.

We can experience such scenarios quite often. We try to focus on something or someone, but it doesn't work. Focusing is hard. With electronic devices demanding our attention, and the abundance of information hitting us every second, it can be hard to dial down and focus. Thankfully, there are some scientifically proven methods that can help us increase focus in the long run.

THE POWER of the Chewing Gum

What if I told you that chewing gum could actually help your focus? Something as simple as gum doesn't seem like it could really help a lot, but it actually can. Whether you're a bubble-gum lover or a spearmint-obsessed chewer, any kind of gum can help you to improve your focus. This is something that has been studied in-depth among researchers. A gum costs pennies and it could improve focus. I'm sold.

In the British Journal of Psychology, researchers found that chewing gum helps focus because it increases the amount of oxygen that flows to the parts of the brain that are responsible for attention. More oxygen improves your brain's function, so it could literally save you from daydreaming during that

important class or meeting you're attending.

Another study performed by Lucy Wilkinson and Andrew Scholey found that gum gives your insulin levels a small spike, which gives your brain an added energy boost and improves long-term memory. This is all just from chewing gum!

If you aren't completely convinced, don't worry. I'm not done yet. Another team of psychologists at St. Lawrence University did a study about how chewing gum would affect a group of individuals during demanding cognitive tasks. There were 159 students that were given these tasks. Things like logic puzzles, random number sequences, and other challenging brain games were required in this study. Half of the group got gum and half of the group didn't. The group that was given gum was separated further into sugar-free gum and sugar-added gum.

What researchers found was that in five out of six different tests, the group that was chewing the gum outperformed the group that wasn't. However, whether the gum was filled with sugar or not didn't matter. You could potentially chew any type of gum you want and perform better during the day while working or attending something important. Just by grabbing your favorite flavor, you increase your focus. If you want to develop good focus habits, start out by trying to chew some gum. I wish someone showed this study to my teachers back in the day.

THE SOUND of Silence

If you're not a huge gum chewer, there are other alternatives to making your focus better and stronger. One way to improve your focus is to engage in something we all probably know, but many of us don't like to do.

Quiet time.

Being in silence has been shown to be better for our focus. Now, I know what a lot of you are thinking. Many of us claim that it is impossible to get work done in the silence because our mind wanders too much during it. I'm not necessarily talking about some soothing music in the background. Although that could also distract you, I'm talking about ambient noise, like cars honking their horns, kids screaming outside, and other noises that you don't necessarily expect to happen. Sudden loud sounds release the hormone cortisol which is best known for producing the "fight or flight" response in us evolutionarily. Back in the hunter-gatherer days cortisol was a means of survival, helping us react to what could be a life- threatening situation. Cortisol therefore, according to the former director of Lake Erie College of Osteopathic Medicine, Mark A.W. Andrews, can hinder your ability to focus and do good work. Your brain gets busy with strategizing survival

pathways.

If you live on a busy street in New York, horns honking are probably second nature to you. But that doesn't mean they don't affect you. Design your workspace to reflect the ambient noise so it doesn't disturb your work in its entirety. Maybe this means you need to embrace the noise. Choose some relaxing music that you know you can tune out and focus through. The music can stop the sudden noises from grabbing your attention, and you can remain focused throughout it.

White noise, counterintuitively, can be quite useful in enhancing focus when you can't get rid of street sounds. "The notion has surfaced that it might be beneficial to mask distracting sounds by playing white noise (…) White noise is a random mixture of sound frequencies that when heard in low volume can improve detection of a simultaneous isolated signal with equal power of any frequency. Perhaps this is because the presence of a homogenous signal (white noise) improves the contrast with a novel superimposed signal. A contributing factor might be the brain's usual response of habituating to a constant stimulus, effectively creating an empty-stimulus state in which other stimuli would be augmented,"[5] said Adrian Furnham and Lisa Strbac of University College, London.

If you can, try working in places like libraries where it's often quiet, and you can even blend in with the smooth tones of a local coffee shop. Using these noises to your advantage will help you focus better.

If you work remotely like me, you can rent a working space. There are buildings specified to offer you this facility. You pay an amount of money monthly, but in return, you get a polished office, free coffee – in better places, even Cheerios – and you can work in peace and quiet. It is also proven through research that it is healthy to separate your workspace from your home. So if you have a home office, work remotely, or have your own business without an office, renting a workspace is not only a good idea noise-wise, but also psychologically. To put it simply, it is easier to leave your work-related problems at the office if you actually have one.

THE GOOD OLD Meditation

Speaking of quiet, another way to increase your focus is with a little bit of meditation. The Psychological Science journal recently came out with a study that showed meditation can help people focus their attention on whatever task it is that they are doing – even if it is incredibly boring.

It was led by Katherine MacLean of UC Davis and included twelve other researchers. They noticed that almost everyone gets tired after concentrating on a task. It exerts a lot of brain power, and the exhaustion sets in. The boring task that the participants had to do was to watch lines pop up on a computer screen. Whenever a smaller line popped up, they had to press down on their mouse. It was incredibly boring, and that was the point of it all. However, some of the participants had meditated at the retreat before this task.

Those who had meditated were much better at seeing the subtle differences in the lines, and their ability to find the smaller lines increased with the amount of meditation they were doing. This study showed that meditation can help you to focus and perform better, but there was one caveat. The meditators didn't react any faster to the tasks than those who hadn't meditated. While they were more accurate and better at it, they were not faster.

DOODLING MOOD (LING)

There are so many benefits of meditation, but so many of us refuse to do it, regardless. To some peace doesn't equate with staying still, there's actually nothing more stressing to them. They like being in some kind of motion. If you fall into that boat, doodling might be a better way to help you focus. Jackie Andrade performed a study asking the participants to doodle through the recordings. The ones who doodled while listening to the recordings had a much higher retention level than those who were not doodling.

We used to get chastised for doodling in elementary school, but it actually helped us to increase our focus. Doodling takes just enough of our attention that we don't wander off into daydreams, so we stay focused on the task at hand. These can be doodling simple lines or small pictures, but it should help you focus more on what you are hearing. Obviously, there are some times when doodling won't work. When your vision is needed, you'd be better off trying out a different focus habit than doodling. However, if you're in on a phone meeting or just need to listen to something, doodling can help to make things clearer, easier to understand, and give you a better retention rate.

THE MAGIC of Nature

When I was a kid, I lived in the countryside among green fields, rushing rivers, chickens, cows, and bugs. I felt I was one with the nature. After the age of fifteen, I became a big-city girl, which meant that I would spend a bunch of time inside stuffy buildings. I would spend hours upon hours sitting in lectures, studying in my dorm, and socializing indoors. Even though there was plenty to see and do outdoors, I stayed inside. It wasn't until my second semester that I realized something had to change.

I felt overwhelmed being surrounded by walls all the time; living in my private prison with the doors open. I suddenly felt claustrophobic and not ready to spend another minute inside. I took a deep breath and decided to venture outdoors, unsure of what I would find. Thankfully, the winter was melting away and a few cherry blossom trees had started to bloom with the warm spring air. I wasn't sure what I wanted to do outdoors, but just the feeling of being outside left me refreshed. It was a bit later that I decided to take a walk around campus and then settle into one of the outdoor picnic tables to finish my studying. After that, I was hooked. Any moment I could spend outside was a good moment. I felt relieved and rejuvenated, and my work reflected it. The assignments I turned in were better, and studying became easier. The tranquil sounds of nature had gotten to me, and I felt like I had missed out on nature by not discovering it until now.

Our lives are busy but we don't need to be busy indoors all the time. We know that we should spend some time outdoors to get that vitamin D from the sun, but how often do we really do it? Instead, we pop some vitamins and hope that will help us live out our lives.

It turns out that there's a big reason you should be spending more time outdoors. Believe it or not, looking at green stuff is beneficial for our focus. And where can you find green stuff? Outdoors! In a study done at the University of Melbourne, Kate Lee and a group of researchers looked at how interrupting a tedious or attention-demanding task with a 40-second micro-break would affect the results. The micro-break they used was having the participants look at a picture of a green roof. What they found was that just looking at this green roof improved focus and performance on the task. The participants also made fewer mistakes.

So while looking at something green can help to improve your focus, there's nothing better than looking outside and seeing some trees. However, if you can't get up and walk around to get this break to work for you, consider adding a few plants or succulents to your home or office to bring nature to you. It's a simple thing that can help you to feel more grounded and at peace.

NATURAL LIGHTS

Another way to bring nature to you is to work in natural light.

We are under the scrutiny of artificial light all day long, and it isn't good for us. Northwestern University did a study that found a correlation between the lighting the person used and how well they slept, their activity levels, and their quality of life. The employees who worked in natural light slept an additional 46 minutes a night, slept more soundly, and reported a higher quality of life.

Not having natural light can mess with your body's circadian rhythm. This is what tells you it is time to sleep and wake during the day and night. It's also responsible for alerting you about meal times and other daily activities. Disruptions to this can cause abnormal sleep patterns, but it can also cause depression and lethargy. It is a serious concern for many, and just switching out your lighting can help to reduce this problem.

A study published in The Responsible Workplace concluded that windows were the number one deciding factor of the occupants' level of satisfaction with the building. Just imagine how much better you feel when there is a window near to you, as opposed to you sitting in a room with no windows at all. Natural lighting makes happier workers because it affects our mood and behavior. There were also fewer illnesses found in people who were exposed to natural light during the day, and that increases efficiency and productivity levels as well. Bright light can also help reduce cortisol levels, something that is responsible for our stress.

If you have a window near you, open the blinds and let the sun shine on your workplace. However, if you aren't near a window, try and take a few breaks during the day where you can go outside and sit for a moment in the sunshine. It will help you perform better, but it will also make you a much happier person. And who is anyone to argue with that, right?

GO GREEN

As I mentioned briefly earlier, plants are another way to increase productivity and bring nature to you. There was a study conducted in the Netherlands and UK that randomly assigned employees to work with some plants in their vicinity. The ones who had a plant near them outperformed the employees who didn't have any access to plants. It seems like a minor detail, but there are actually a lot of reasons as to why plants can help us to feel better.

Humans used to spend a lot of time outdoors, and only recently has that changed. Plants are a way to connect with the past and still feel like we can be outside. There's more to it than that, though. Plants can also improve air quality because they literally suck some toxins from the air. This leads to a perception that the air quality is better because of plants, but it also makes the environment more visually appealing. There's nothing that a few flowers or succulents can't do to liven up a room. What goes from a boring office cubicle then turns into a wonderful oasis that is filled with fresh and clean air because of the plants around you. Plus, you don't even have to have them right next to you. Just seeing a plant is close to you can help you perform better during the day. There's no reason to say no to having plants near you!

OH, Those Cute YouTube Videos

Last, but certainly not least, is a method that can help you perform better throughout the day. You'll never believe it... but looking at baby animals can actually improve your focus and performance. I know, you're probably thinking this is a bunch of nonsense, but I'm not joking here!

We all love baby animals, so rejoice in the fact that there are benefits from looking at them. In a Japanese research paper, The Power of Kawaii: Viewing Cute Images Promotes a Careful.

Behavior and Attentional Focus, researchers found that looking at cute images at work can help boost your attention and overall performance. Three groups of students played a game, and then looked at a few images before playing the game again. The group that had to look at baby animals outperformed their peers by a very significant margin. Apparently, it could be connected to a nurturing instinct that we all seem to have. Something about those cute animals just makes it difficult for us to not pay attention.

We've all been on the Internet and have cooed over the adorable baby animals, but now you don't need to feel bad about it if you're sneaking a peek at the baby panda at work. If anyone walks in to say something, tell them that science has actually proved that looking at baby animals improves your performance. Sure, they might think you're a little nutty, but it's the truth! Between all of these different little ways to improve your performance, you should be a working machine when you need to focus on a task.

5. 50 QUICK DAILY ROUTINE CHANGES

1. Slow down.
2. Stop once a day to admire something around you.
3. Find the positive equivalent of all your negative thoughts. (Example: Life's hard – life's easy. I can't do it – I can do it.)
4. Make walking your daily routine. Walk for at least 30 minutes each day just for the sake of walking.
5. One apple a day keeps the doctor away. Did you know that ripe apples smile? After you eat them, they transfer their smile to you.
6. Drink at least 2 liters (68 fl. oz.) a day.
7. Start your morning with a tall glass of room temperature water.
8. Learn to meditate, and do it for at least 10 minutes before sleeping.
9. Use the evening meditation to forgive yourself and others.
10. Spend time in nature. The more, the better.
11. Smile, and the world will smile back at you.
12. Have a heartfelt laugh each day.
13. Give at least three compliments a day.
14. Look in the mirror and tell yourself that you're beautiful.

15. Call your mother. (Or father, son, daughter, or anyone close to you.)
16. Read something new for 10-15 minutes each day.
17. Find the possibilities around you. See opportunities where others don't.
18. Choose to master a skill and dedicate a few minutes to it each day.
19. Search for the lesson in each failure.
20. Before making an important decision, think about two more reasons why you should or shouldn't do it, besides the obvious.
21. Focus on the solution, not the problem.
22. Stretch every morning.
23. Create your success. Don't expect it to find you.
24. Ask questions frequently.
25. Instead of judging people, try to find common ground with them.
26. If you did something wrong, apologize quickly and move on. Don't look for excuses, but don't hate yourself.
27. Don't try to be busy. That's a sign of a life that lacks organization and control.
28. Use what you have now instead of procrastinating a day with the hope that you'll be better tomorrow.
29. Step one is not the planning and preparation. Step one is hands-on action.
30. There is no "right time." There is only now or never.
31. Don't let your life stop and start. Flow.
32. Take calculated risks.
33. Be proactive instead of reactive.
34. Improve your communication skills.
35. Improve your emotion-handling skills.
36. Identify your core values and act according to them.
37. Help someone else each day.

38. Don't take anything for granted.

39. Practice poverty at least one day a month – eat cheap food, wear old clothing. See your greatest fears became reality and realize they are not as horrible as they may seem.

40. The strongest and smartest aren't the best at surviving; those who can adapt to changing circumstances are.

41. Play sports, not (only) for the sake of looking good, but feeling good as well.

42. Embrace constructive criticism and feedback.

43. Keep yourself away from people who bring you down.

44. Relaxing doesn't mean you stopped moving. Healthy breaks are part of the flow.

45. You are not your job. Your career is not your identity. It is what you do. Your spouse and children are not your life – they complement it to perfection.

46. Practice what you preach.

47. Green is good: eat more green food, drink green tea, go out in a green environment, and cross the street only when the light is green for you.

48. Stay true to your beliefs. Don't change them for anybody's sake, just your own.

49. Eat walnuts. They look like a brain for a reason.

50. Print these 50 life-improving steps and read them each morning.

FINAL THOUGHTS

I hope you feel empowered with new weapons to defeat procrastination, become more productive, and develop new daily routines based on new perspectives from alternative philosophies, and you know what you need to do to focus better. Now you just have to practice.

I wish to leave you with a few more nuggets of information to help you stay on track.

- **Focus on what you want.** Many people concentrate on what they want to avoid. They do not want to be overweight anymore. They do not want to cause an accident. Focus on what you want, not on what you don't want.

- **Make your goal irresistible.** Don't just say to yourself, "Yep, I want to be slim, strong, energetic, and rich…" Instead, use something like: "I want to burst with energy. I will be more active, I will be stronger, and I will be an example to my kids/my family/my friends." You need to envision your goal so clearly that it makes you take the first steps. Create an image that pulls you toward it. Make the goal so irresistible that you immediately want to get started reaching it and developing that particular area.

Your quality of life will improve because you are excited about where you are headed. Your adrenaline levels will increase suddenly, and that's a good feeling.

- **Find the best tools.** Find the path to reaching your goal and solving the problem. If it doesn't exist, you have to build it. Find the starting point. Create it, if there isn't one. It is great if you are enthusiastic and focused. However, it doesn't matter how focused you are and what you believe in if you are using the wrong tools. The wrong strategy or an inappropriate map won't get you closer to your goal, either.

You can find good tools if you imitate someone who is successful at something you want to be successful at. If you emulate someone, you can save time, energy, and money. If you know someone with outstanding results who is already successful, why would you want to reinvent the wheel?

Success always leaves lasting traces. Find the very best in your field, see what they do and how they do it, and copy them. Develop your own style and monitor the process. Adjust what is already working instead of conducting time-consuming experiments.

- Resolve your inner conflicts. Several forces are fighting with each other when there is an internal conflict. You are the one who can use these forces to your benefit. Inner conflicts are often caused by the lack of knowing your "why." Why do you want what you want? Why do you want that particular goal?

You might think that being successful and making a lot of money is immoral, not spiritual. Maybe you value spirituality and financial success doesn't seem to go well with it.

How can we resolve these inner conflicts and unleash the power of their forces? There is only one way: identify the most important thing for you to do today.

Do not make a decision based on what others expect you to do, or what happened in your past; what your parents, friends, or society wants is irrelevant. When you identify the conflict, bring the values you represent into harmony with your life. Be in agreement with the things that are most important to you.

You will see that, once you are in harmony with yourself, you will resolve your inner conflict.

Do not stop there. Pass your knowledge on. Help others. Show others what you have and what you have learned. When you teach others, you share your contentment and the joy that comes with success.

I believe in you!

Yours truly,

Made in the USA
Monee, IL
28 December 2022